THE LITTLE BOOK OF
AVOCADO
TIPS

Andrew Langley

THE LITTLE BOOK OF
AVOCADO
TIPS

Andrew Langley

A.

The name [avocado] comes from
the Nahuatl word *ahuacatl*, which
was apparently inspired by the fruit's
pear-like shape and irregular surface:
it means 'testicle'.

Harold McGee (b.1951), American
writer on food science

1. **Look out for unusual varieties of avocado. The overwhelming bestseller is the Hass** variety – dark green and warty skinned with a fatty, oily flesh. **But there are plenty of others** (if you can find them). Try Zutano, which has a light and lemony flavour, or Fuerte which is nutty and creamy, or Pinkerton, which is even richer than Hass.

"Look out for unusual varieties of avocado. The overwhelming bestseller is the Hass ... but there are plenty of others."

2. How do you pick the perfect avocado in a store? Shop owners don't like us squeezing their fruit – which are often wrapped in plastic anyway. The only way to judge is by eye. **Choose an avocado with a shiny skin, with no discoloration and no flattened areas.** It should look firm and healthy all over.

"Choose an avocado with a shiny skin, with no discoloration and no flattened areas."

3. When you get it home, **just put your avocado in a bowl in the kitchen and** keep it away from excessive light and heat; 15–24°C is perfect. Otherwise **leave it to ripen naturally** for up to a week.

"Just put your avocado in a bowl in the kitchen and leave it to ripen naturally."

4. **Keep unripe avocados out of the fridge.** They are warm-climate fruits, and chilling can shock them into never ripening at all. On the other hand, **ripe avocados can be kept in a fridge for several days without spoiling.**

"Keep unripe avocados out of the fridge. Ripe avocados can be kept in a fridge for several days without spoiling."

5. **How do you tell when an avocado is perfectly ripe?** Give it a gentle push with a finger. It should give slightly. Next try to pull out the little stem stub. If it falls out easily, and the flesh underneath is green, the avocado is ready to eat. If it stays put, leave the fruit for another day or so.

"How do you tell when an avocado is perfectly ripe?"

6. **Avocados slow to soften up? Store them in a paper** (not plastic) **bag with a couple of other ripe fruits,** such as apples or bananas (still at room temperature). These naturally give off an ethylene gas which speeds up the ripening process.

"Avocados slow to soften up? Store them in a paper bag with a couple of other ripe fruits."

7. It's easy to cut an avocado safely. Just concentrate! First, remove the stem stub. Then **press the avocado onto a chopping board** with the palm of one hand. Use a sharp knife to **slice down the centre of the fruit, cutting lengthways round the stone.** Finally, grip the avocado on each side of the cut and twist in opposite directions.

"Press the avocado onto a chopping board ... slice down the centre of the fruit, cutting lengthways round the stone."

8. **One half always contains the stone. So what's the best way to remove it?** Hold the half avocado on a board. Get a big sharp knife and tap, rather than chop, the blade on the stone (with fingers well out of the way). When the blade is wedged into the stone, twist the knife horizontally and – hey presto!

"One half always contains the stone. So what's the best way to remove it?"

9. An avocado rots faster than most other fruit. Once cut, it will quickly go brown. To slow this process down, **rub the cut side with lemon or lime juice. Cover with clingfilm to stop oxygen reaching the flesh.**

"Rub the cut side with lemon or lime juice. Cover with clingfilm to stop oxygen reaching the flesh."

10.

Even when an avocado is so overripe that it is mushy or patched with brown, it's still fine to eat. Whizz it up in soups, smoothies, sorbets and many other great dishes. Only avoid fruit which smells funny or has mouldy spots. Chuck it on the compost heap.

Even when an avocado is so overripe that it is mushy or patched with brown, it's still fine to eat.

11. **Glory in green, and make use of the avocado's stunning colour.** Crush with a fork and mix into mashed potato or chickpea hummus. Best of all, stir it into some scrambled eggs just before they firm up, along with crumbly goat's cheese.

Glory in green, and make use of the avocado's stunning colour.

12.

Sliced avocado has a thousand uses, from highlights in salads to a heavenly accompaniment for smoked salmon. Halve and de-stone the fruit. Peel away the rough skin from each half (a small knife is fine for this). Lay the halves on a board and slice lengthways.

Sliced avocado has a thousand uses...

13.

Avocados can taste bitter when cooked, but you can still make avocado soup. Gently sauté a chopped onion and garlic clove in olive oil. Then put in a blender with 1 mashed avocado (overripe is OK), 1 litre of chicken stock and the juice of a lemon. Whizz up, season, cool and serve with chopped parsley and a blob of creme fraiche.

"Avocados can taste bitter when cooked, but you can still make avocado soup."

14.

Avocado and fish #1: with sardines on toast. Avocados marry very happily with many kinds of fish. Drain 2 tins of sardines and marinate for 1 hour in olive oil and vinegar. Grill slices of stale bread and brush with the vinaigrette. Top with thinly sliced avocado, chopped shallots and the sardines. Eat at once.

"Avocado and fish #1: with sardines on toast."

15.

Among avocado dishes, **guacamole is the guv'nor.** Even so, there's nothing like a definitive recipe for this celebrated dip. **Here's a very simple and fresh-tasting version.** Mash up the flesh of 1 avocado with a crushed garlic clove, the juice of half a lemon, chopped coriander, and salt and pepper to taste. Get dipping.

"Guacomole is the guv'nor... Here's a very simple and fresh-tasting version..."

16.

For a spicier, subtler guacamole, take the recipe from page 34 (maybe substituting lime for lemon juice) and add the following. For every avocado, **add 1 finely chopped green chilli and 1 small sliced spring onion**. Mix this all in a stone mortar, **and gently add 1 small peeled and diced tomato.**

"For a spicier, subtler guacamole, add 1 finely chopped green chilli and 1 small sliced spring onion, and gently add 1 small peeled and diced tomato."

17. **Poor man's butter, or *mantequilla de pobre*,** is another fine Mexican invention. It is a slightly sloppier version of guacamole, made simply by mashing together avocado flesh, chopped tomatoes, olive oil, lime juice, salt and pepper. It **makes a heavenly dip for plain grilled chunks of lean pork.**

"Poor man's butter, or *mantequilla de pobre*, makes a heavenly dip for plain grilled chunks of lean pork."

18.

Use avocado oil for high temperature frying. It has a much higher smoke point than most common oils, including olive oil and flaxseed oil (which smoke at a relatively low heat). **And** with its high level of fatty acid and low levels of saturated fats, avocado oil **is also a much healthier option** than cheaper corn and soy oils.

"Use avocado oil for high temperature frying. It has a much higher smoke point and is also a much healthier option."

19.

Avocado lifts a lime sorbet into the stratosphere. Mix a cup each of water and white sugar and boil up into a syrup. Add the zest from 3 limes and chill. In a blender, combine the flesh of 3 avocados with the juice from the limes, plus salt and a tin of creamed coconut. Fold in the syrup and freeze, stirring occasionally.

"Avocado lifts a lime sorbet into the stratosphere."

20.

Everyone knows **avocados are ridiculously good for you, but how about tripling that megaton healthiness by adding banana and blueberries in one big smoothie?** In a blender, whizz up 1 frozen banana, the flesh of 1 avocado, plus 2 cups of blueberries. Add iced water until you get the right consistency.

"Avocados are ridiculously good for you, but how about tripling that megaton healthiness by adding banana and blueberries in one big smoothie?"

21.

Avocado and fish #2: skate with avocado mayonnaise. Poach the skate in water with 1 bay leaf and peppercorns for 15 minutes, When it's cool, take off the skin and cartilaginous bits. Toss the flesh with a chopped avocado, a peeled and chopped tomato and cubes of boiled potato. Mix in some home-made mayonnaise.

"Avocado and fish #2: skate with avocado mayonnaise."

22. Mozzarella and avocado are perfect partners. The slight springiness and sourness of the cheese contrasts beautifully with the avocado's unctuousness. **For a quick scrumptious salad mix together good quality sliced mozzarella and sliced avocado, and add chopped tomato.** Drizzle with olive oil and balsamic vinegar.

"For a quick scrumptious salad mix together good quality sliced mozzarella and avocado, and add chopped tomato."

23.

Recipes for avocado toast would fill at least 20 of these little books. **The basis is utterly simple: spread mashed avocado on hot toast, maybe with a little oil, lemon juice and ground pepper.** After this you can add bacon, chopped mango, crumbled feta, creamed cashew, flaked tuna, sundried tomato, scrambled egg – use your imagination.

"The basis is utterly simple: spread mashed avocado on hot toast, maybe with a little oil, lemon juice and ground pepper. "

24. **Deep-frying avocados does wonders for the texture but little for the flavour.** So **use a batter which includes wheat flour and corn flour, and lighten it with beer.** Season the avocado slices and drop gently into hot oil. Fry for a few minutes then remove, drain on paper and salt again. Serve in tortillas with tomato and chilli salsa.

"Deep-frying avocados does wonders for the texture but little for the flavour. Use a batter which includes wheat flour and corn flour, and lighten it with beer. "

25.

Guasacaca **is a Venezuelan sauce served as a dip with grilled meat, empanadas and even sandwiches.** Chop 3 avocados, half a red pepper, 1 onion, 3 garlic cloves, 1 green chilli and a fistful of parsley. Blend all these along with wine vinegar, olive oil and seasoning. **It's very different from the usual guacamole.**

Guasacaca is a Venezuelan sauce served as a dip with grilled meat, empanadas and even sandwiches. It's very different from the usual guacamole.

26.

Avocados were made for baking eggs. Cut one in half, remove the stone and scoop out a little extra flesh. Break an egg in a cup and spoon the unbroken yolk into one half of the avocado. Add as much white as will fit. Repeat for the other half and bake both at 180°C for 15–20 minutes or until just set, depending on how you like your eggs. Serve with sautéed chorizo and some rocket.

"Avocados were made for baking eggs."

27.

Here's a creamy sauce to go with spicy chicken. Season 2 chicken breasts with salt, cumin and a dash of cayenne pepper, and brown both sides in oil. Add a 400g tin of chopped tomatoes and cook for another 10 minutes. Remove the chicken and reduce the juices. Off the heat, add diced avocado, chopped parsley and a dollop of sour cream.

"Here's a creamy sauce to go with spicy chicken..."

28.

Avocado and fish #3: smoked salmon with avocado and horseradish sauce. Spread a single layer of smoked salmon on a large plate. Drizzle sparingly with horseradish sauce (preferably homemade). Scatter diced avocado and red onion on top, with a sprinkling of chopped chives and chervil.

"Avocado and fish #3: smoked salmon with avocado and horseradish sauce."

29. **Grapefruit is yet another perfect partner for avocado.** For a zingy salad, slice an avocado lengthways, toss in vinaigrette and arrange in a circle on a dish. Peel a pink grapefruit and divide into segments. Put them in the centre of the dish and drizzle with more vinaigrette. Serve chilled with lobster or crab.

"Grapefruit is yet another perfect partner for avocado.

30.

Lightly bitter foods highlight the avocado's creaminess. Here's a very speedy cold soup for a hot day, made of avocado and cucumber. Blend an avocado with a peeled and de-seeded cucumber. Add lemon juice, plus salt and pepper to taste.

"Lightly bitter foods highlight the avocado's creaminess. Here's a very speedy cold soup for a hot day, made of avocado and cucumber...

31.

Start the day with an avocado omelette. Whisk 2 eggs with a dash of water and seasoning. Melt a knob of butter in a frying pan, and at a fair heat pour in the egg mix. After a minute, sprinkle the top with half a cubed avocado, a grating of Cheddar cheese and shards of crispy bacon. Fold over and serve with a spicy tomato salsa.

Start the day with an avocado omelette.

32. **There's no end to great avo salads – try it with beetroot and fennel.** Roast a big golden beetroot in sunflower or vegetable oil until soft (about 1 hour). Peel and slice and put on a dish. Add a sliced avocado, a (very thinly) sliced fennel bulb and a scattering of rocket. Drizzle on a mustard vinaigrette and top with ricotta.

"There's no end to great avo salads – try it with beetroot and fennel."

33.

Bake an avocado with salty blue cheese. **Mix together** 100g **Roquefort** cheese, 50g **chopped walnuts**, 1 **egg** and tablespoons of **cream and breadcrumbs. Spoon into avocado halves and bung in the oven** at 180°C for 15 minutes. Serve with a tomato and rosemary salad.

"Mix together Roquefort, chopped walnuts, egg, cream and breadcrumbs. Spoon into avocado halves and bung in the oven."

34.

Avocado gives this quick soda bread a magic twist. In a bowl combine 220g wholemeal flour, 50g brown sugar, 1 big teaspooon of baking powder, 1 small teaspoon of baking soda and the same of salt. Mix in 1 avocado mashed with 220ml buttermilk and a beaten egg. Add a handful of torn basil leaves and bake at 180°C for 40 minutes.

"Avocado gives this quick soda bread a magic twist..."

35. **Avocado and fish #4: *feroce d'avocat*.** 'Fierce avocado' is a fish starter from the French Antilles. Blend 450g of soaked and poached salt cod with parsley, the flesh of 1 avocado, lime juice and a habanero chilli (you choose the strength). Then stir in 450g of cassava flour and oil. Chill and serve.

"Avocado and fish #4: *feroce d'avocat.*"

36. **Ripe avocado can be frozen to retain flavour** (if not – wholly – texture). Cut the flesh into cubes and put in the freezer, spread out on a sheet of baking paper. When they're frozen, transfer to a plastic tub. They'll last for 3 months. Defrost gradually in a bowl of cold water for 10 minutes.

Ripe avocados can be frozen to retain flavour.

37.

Grow your own avocado plant.
Take the stone from a ripe fruit and insert 4 wooden toothpicks, evenly spaced, so they stick out midway up the long side. Place the stone, pointy side up, over a glass of water. After a month or so, the stone should split and roots and a shoot appear. Plant this with compost and grit in a pot. Water often.

"Grow your own avocado plant."

38.

Make a simple hand cream and moisturiser based on avocado oil.

Place a small bowl over a pan of hot water. In this, melt down some pieces of beeswax and mix with avocado oil. Add a few drops of essential oils such as orange, rose or lavender. Pour the cream into a jar to cool.

"Make a simple hand cream and moisturiser based on avocado oil...

39.

Avocado leaves may be harder to find than the fruit, but they **are worth searching for.** Use them as herbs, which give a subtle nutty aniseed flavour. **Toast the leaves gently in the oven and** crush them with a rolling pin. **Add them when cooking fish dishes, soups and bean stews.**

"Avocado leaves are worth searching for. Toast the leaves gently in the oven and add them when cooking fish dishes, soups and bean stews."

40.

Creamy green margarita anybody?
In a blender put 2 measures of lime juice, 1 of tequila, a big slosh of Cointreau and the flesh of 2 avocados. Fill up with crushed ice. Whizz it all together until smooth, and serve in a glass rimmed with salt and topped with a lime slice.

"Creamy green margarita anybody?"

41.

Here's a quick and easy avocado lemon cake. Whisk up 4 eggs and 220g sugar until fluffy. In a big bowl sift together 450g white flour, the flesh of 2 avocados, the zest of 1 lemon and 1 heaped teaspoon of baking powder. Fold in the eggy mixture and bake for 45 minutes at 170°C. Top with a lemony icing when cool.

"Here's a quick and easy avocado lemon cake..."

42.

Avocado gives perfect silkiness to a mousse. **For a heavenly raw chocolate mousse, just whizz together a banana, an avocado, 4 tablespoons raw cacao powder, 2 tablespoons honey and 1 teaspoon of sea salt.** Add a little coconut oil to lubricate. Put in glasses and chill for an hour – if you can wait!

"For a heavenly raw chocolate mousse, just whizz together a banana, an avocado, 4 tablespoons raw cacao powder, 2 tablespoons honey and 1 teaspoon of salt salt."

43.

The avolatte began as a joke – but it **is still the whackiest way to serve coffee. Take half an avocado** and **scoop out the flesh.** Place the empty skin on a saucer **and pour in a single espresso** coffee. Top with steamed and frothed milk.

"The avolatte is still the whackiest way to serve coffee. Take half an avocado, scoop out the flesh and pour in a single espresso."

44.

The very best way to eat an avocado is still the simplest. Enjoy it for what it is – a complete food with a delicate taste all of its own. Just take 1 perfectly ripe fruit, cut it in half and remove the stone. **Put the halves on a plate, and sprinkle with sea salt and pepper. Pour over a little olive oil and a dash of balsamic vinegar. That's it.**

"Put the halves on a plate, and sprinkle with sea salt and pepper. Pour over a little olive oil and a dash of balsamic vinegar. That's it."

45.

Babies love avocado puree. It's pure, mild, skinless – and rich in Omega-3. What's more, it's green. To serve it, just mash up the flesh and thin down with a little water. You can also add some mashed banana to make it even more nutritious.

"Babies love avocado puree. It's pure, mild, skinless – and rich in Omega 3."

46.

Abuzz with minerals and vitamins, slick with unsaturated fats, cheap and chemical-free – **avocados make a perfect skin tonic.** So make this amazingly simple avocado and honey face mask. **Mash up the flesh of an avocado with 1 tablespoon of honey till smooth. Apply to the face and leave for 15 minutes** before washing off in warm water.

"Avocados make a perfect skin tonic. Mash up the flesh of an avocado with 1 tablespoon of honey till smooth. Apply to the face and leave for 15 minutes."

47. **Avocado is great for your hair** – especially for moisturising dry or frizzy locks. **Whizz up the flesh of 1 avocado with** 4 tablespoons of **extra virgin olive oil**, 6 tablespoons of **shea butter and** 2 tablespoons of **cider vinegar** (add more oil if necessary). Wet the hair, apply the mixture and put on a shower cap. Rinse it out after 30 minutes.

"Avocado is great for your hair. Whizz up the flesh of 1 avocado with extra virgin olive oil, shea butter and cider vinegar."

48. **Too much sun? An avocado can fix that too.** Mash half an avocado with 1 tablespoon of aloe vera and dab the mixture gently on the sunburnt areas. It will quickly ease the skin and relieve the pain.

"Too much sun? An avocado can fix that too."

49. **Soothe stomach ache with a simple avocado stone tea.** Slice the stone in half lengthways (carefully!), drop into a cup and pour on boiling water. Steep for 10 minutes, then remove the halves. Drink the infusion slowly.

"Soothe stomach ache with a simple avocado stone tea."

50. **Massage sore feet with avocados (the stones, at least).** Save the stones from half a dozen fruits and put them in a tray or large bowl. Then kick off your shoes and roll the soles of your feet about in them. **The hard, oily surface and smooth round shape give a perfect massage.**

"Massage sore feet with avocados (the stones, at least). The hard, oily surface and smooth round shape give a perfect massage."

Andrew Langley

Andrew Langley is **a knowledgeable food and drink writer.** Among his formative influences he lists a season picking grapes in Bordeaux, several years of raising sheep and chickens in Wiltshire and two decades drinking his grandmother's tea. He has written books on a number of Scottish and Irish whisky distilleries and is the editor of the highly regarded anthology of the writings of the legendary Victorian chef Alexis Soyer.

"A knowledgeable food and drink writer."

Little Books of Tips from
Absolute Press

Aga	Gardening
Allotment	Gin
Avocado	Golf
Beer	Herbs
Cake Decorating	Spice
Cheese	Tea
Coffee	Whisky
Fishing	Wine

If you enjoyed this book, try...

THE LITTLE BOOK OF

HERB

TIPS

"As well as having a deliciously citric taste, the fleshy leaves of purslane are a rich source of iron and Omega-3.

"Chervil adds a heavenly touch to uncompicated dishes such as scrambled eggs and omelettes.

ABSOLUTE PRESS

An imprint of Bloomsbury Publishing Plc

50 Bedford Square	1385 Broadway
London	New York
WC1B 3DP	NY 10018
UK	USA

www.bloomsbury.com

ABSOLUTE PRESS and the A. logo are trademarks of Bloomsbury Publishing Plc

First published in 2018

© Andrew Langley, 2018
Cover image: Anna_Shepulova / istockphoto

Andrew Langley has asserted his right under the Copyright, Designs and Patents Act, 1988, to be identified as Author of this work.

A catalogue record for this book is available from the British Library.
Library of Congress Cataloguing-in-Publication data has been applied for.
ISBN 13: 9781472956750

Printed and bound in Spain by Tallers Grafics Soler

D0518673